SEAWORTHY
SONGS

ISBN-13: 978-1-4234-2609-7
ISBN-10: 1-4234-2609-6

HAL•LEONARD®
CORPORATION
7777 W. BLUEMOUND RD. P.O. BOX 13819 MILWAUKEE, WI 53213

Visit Hal Leonard Online at
www.halleonard.com

CONTENTS

BARNACLE BILL THE SAILOR

Words and Music by FRANK LUTHER
and CARSON ROBISON

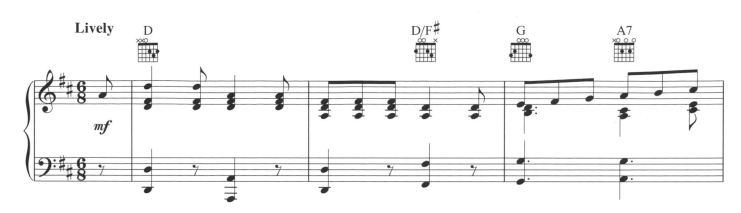

Maiden: 1. "Who's that knock - ing at my door? Who's that knock - ing at my
2. young and hand - some, sir? Are you young and hand-some,
3.-6. *(See additional lyrics)*

door? Who's that knock - ing at my door," cried the fair young maid - en. *Bill:* "It's
sir? Are you young and hand - some, sir?" cried the fair young maid - en. *Bill:* "I'm

4

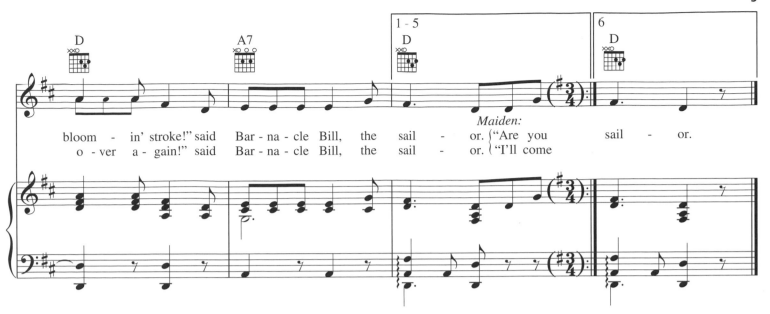

bloom - in' stroke!" said Bar - na - cle Bill, the sail - or. {"Are you sail - or.
o - ver a - gain!" said Bar - na - cle Bill, the sail - or. {"I'll come

Maiden:

Additional Lyrics

3. *Maiden:* "I'll come down and let you in,
   I'll come down and let you in,
   I'll come down and let you in," cried the fair young maiden.
   Bill: "Well, hurry before I bust in the door," said Barnacle Bill, the sailor.
   "I'll rare and tear and rant and roar," said Barnacle Bill, the sailor.
   "I'll spin yuh yarns and tell yuh lies,
   I'll drink your coffee and eat your pies,
   I'll kiss your cheeks and black your eyes," said Barnacle Bill, the sailor.

4. *Maiden:* "Sing me a love song low and sweet,
   Sing me a love song low and sweet,
   Oh! Sing me a love song low and sweet," cried the fair young maiden.
   Bill: "Oh! Sixteen men on a dead man's chest," sang Barnacle Bill, the sailor.
   "Yo he ho and a bottle of rum," sang Barnacle Bill, the sailor.
   "Oh high rig a jig and a jaunting car
   A he a ho are you most done
   Hurray my boys let the bull-jine run!" sang Barnacle Bill, the sailor.

5. *Maiden:* "Tell me that we soon shall wed,
   Tell me that we soon shall wed,
   Tell me that we soon shall wed," cried the fair young maiden.
   Bill: "I've got me a gal in every port!" said Barnacle Bill, the sailor.
   "The handsome gals is what I court!" said Barnacle Bill, the sailor.
   "With my false heart and flatterin' tongue
   I courts 'em all both old and young,
   I courts 'em all and marries none!" said Barnacle Bill, the sailor.

6. *Maiden:* "When shall I see you again?
   When shall I see you again?
   When shall I see you again?" cried the fair young maiden.
   Bill: "Never again I'll come no more!" said Barnacle Bill, the sailor.
   "Tonight I'm sailin' from the shore," said Barnacle Bill, the sailor.
   "If you wait for me to come
   Settin' and waitin' and suckin' yer thumb
   You'll wait until the day of your doom!" said Barnacle Bill, the sailor.
   (Spoken:) "Goodbye."

BEACH BABY

Words and Music by JOHN CARTER
and GILL SHAKESPEARE

Do you re-mem-ber back in old L. A. _____ o _____ oh

when ev-'ry-bod-y drove a Chev-ro-let _____ o _____ oh.

BLUE BAYOU

Words and Music by ROY ORBISON
and JOE MELSON

BEYOND THE SEA

Words and Music by CHARLES TRENET,
ALBERT LASRY and JACK LAWRENCE

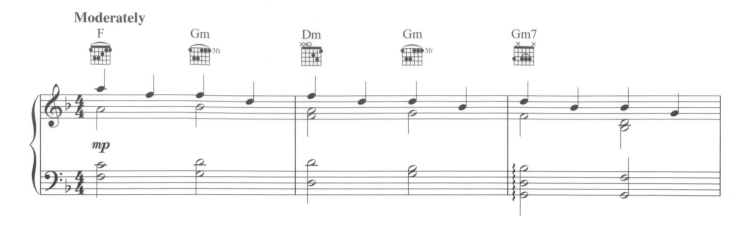

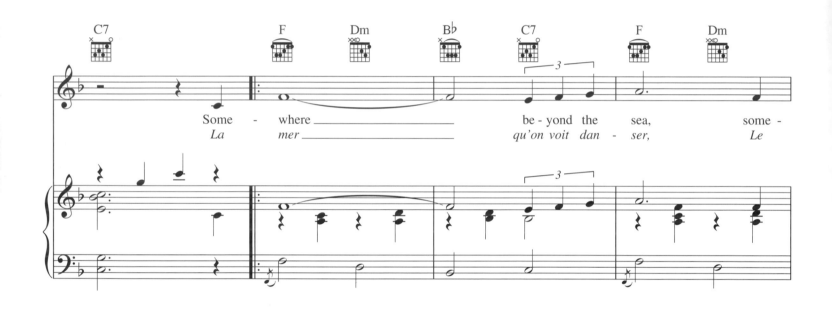

Some - where _____ be - yond the sea, some -
La mer _____ *qu'on voit dan - ser,* *Le*

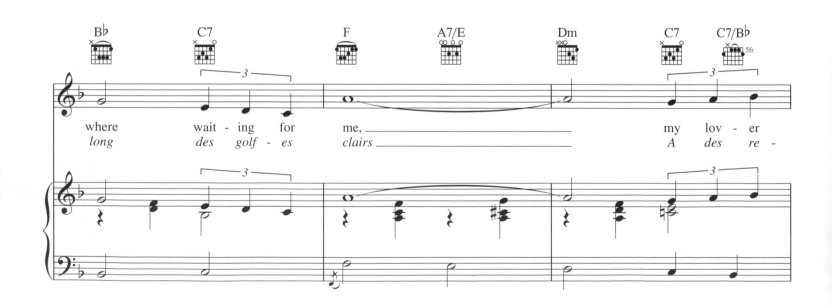

where wait - ing for me, _____ my lov - er
long *des golf - es* *clairs* _____ *A des re -*

COME SAIL AWAY

Words and Music by
DENNIS DeYOUNG

CRY ME A RIVER

Words and Music by
ARTHUR HAMILTON

FERRY 'CROSS THE MERSEY

Words and Music by
GERRARD MARSDEN

HOW DEEP IS THE OCEAN
(How High Is the Sky)

Words and Music by
IRVING BERLIN

I'M POPEYE THE SAILOR MAN

Theme from the Paramount Cartoon POPEYE THE SAILOR

Words and Music by
SAMMY LERNER

ISLAND GIRL

Words and Music by ELTON JOHN
and BERNIE TAUPIN

Moderately fast

I see your teeth flash, Ja- mai-can hon-ey so sweet, down where Lex-ing-ton cross For-ty-sev-enth Street.

ISLANDS IN THE STREAM

Words and Music by BARRY GIBB,
ROBIN GIBB and MAURICE GIBB

Ba - by, when I met you, there was peace un - known. __ I set out to get you with a
I can't live with - out you if the love has gone. __ Ev - 'ry - thing is noth - ing when you

fine - tooth comb. I was soft in - side; __ there __ was some - thing go - ing on. __
got no one, and you walk in the night, __ slow - ly los - ing sight of the

JAMBALAYA
(On the Bayou)

Words and Music by
HANK WILLIAMS

KOKOMO
from the Motion Picture COCKTAIL

Words and Music by MIKE LOVE,
TERRY MELCHER, JOHN PHILLIPS
and SCOTT McKENZIE

Moderately bright

A - ru - ba, Ja - mai - ca, oo ___ I wan - na take ya. Ber -

mu - da, Ba - ha - ma, come ___ on, pret - ty ma - ma. Key Lar - go, Mon - te - go, ba -

- by, why don't we go, Ja - mai - ca. Off the Flor - i - da Keys ___ We'll put out to sea ___

LAZY RIVER

Words and Music by HOAGY CARMICHAEL
and SIDNEY ARODIN

LAUGHTER IN THE RAIN

Words and Music by NEIL SEDAKA
and PHIL CODY

MOON RIVER

from the Paramount Picture BREAKFAST AT TIFFANY'S

Words by JOHNNY MERCER
Music by HENRY MANCINI

MY SHIP

from the Musical Production LADY IN THE DARK

Words by IRA GERSHWIN
Music by KURT WEILL

MY HEART WILL GO ON
(Love Theme from 'Titanic')
from the Paramount and Twentieth Century Fox Motion Picture TITANIC

Music by JAMES HORNER
Lyric by WILL JENNINGS

OL' MAN RIVER

from SHOW BOAT

Lyrics by OSCAR HAMMERSTEIN II
Music by JEROME KERN

OLD CAPE COD

Words and Music by CLAIRE ROTHROCK,
MILT YAKUS and ALLEN JEFFREY

served by a win-dow with an o - cean view, ___ you're sure to fall in love with

old Cape Cod. _____

Wind - ing roads that seem to beck - on you, miles of green be - neath the

skies of blue, church bells chim - ing on a Sun - day morn' re -

ON A SLOW BOAT TO CHINA

By FRANK LOESSER

leave all your lov-ers _____ weep-ing on the far a-way shore. _____
(love-lies) _____

_____ Out on the brin-y _____ with a moon big and

shin-y, _____ melt-ing your heart _____ of stone, _____

_____ I'd love to get you _____ on a slow boat to

ON THE GOOD SHIP LOLLIPOP

from BRIGHT EYES

Words and Music by SIDNEY CLARE
and RICHARD A. WHITING

On the good ship, Lol-li-pop, it's a sweet trip to a can-dy shop, where bon-bons play on the sun-ny beach of pep-per-mint bay. Lem-on-ade stands

OVER THE MOUNTAIN, ACROSS THE SEA

Words and Music by
REX GARVIN

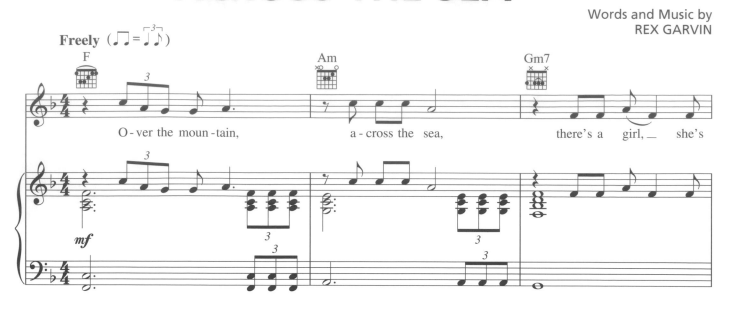

O-ver the moun-tain, a-cross the sea, there's a girl, __ she's

wait-ing just for me. 'Cross o-ver the riv-er, be-yond ev-'ry cloud, __

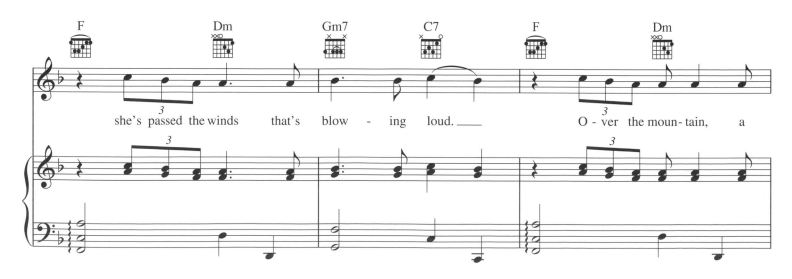

she's passed the winds that's blow-ing loud. __ O-ver the moun-tain, a

RIVERBOAT SHUFFLE

Words and Music by HOAGY CARMICHAEL, MITCHELL PARISH,
IRVING MILLS and DICK VOYNOW

RED SAILS IN THE SUNSET

Words by JIMMY KENNEDY
Music by HUGH WILLIAMS (WILL GROSZ)

RIDE THE WILD SURF

Words and Music by JAN BERRY,
BRIAN WILSON and ROGER CHRISTIAN

RIVER, STAY 'WAY FROM MY DOOR

Written by MORT DIXON
and HARRY WOODS

SAILING

Words and Music by
CHRISTOPHER CROSS

(Sittin' On)
THE DOCK OF THE BAY

Words and Music by STEVE CROPPER
and OTIS REDDING

SEA OF LOVE

Words and Music by GEORGE KHOURY
and PHILIP BAPTISTE

Medium slow Fifties Rock

(1., 3.) Do you re-mem-ber ___ when ___ we met? ___
(2.) Come with me, ___ my ___ love, ___

That's the day ___ I knew you were my pet.
to the sea, ___ the sea ___ of love. ___

I ___ want to tell you how ___ much ___ I
I ___ want to tell you just how ___ much ___ I

SHRIMP BOATS

Words and Music by PAUL MASON HOWARD
and PAUL WESTON

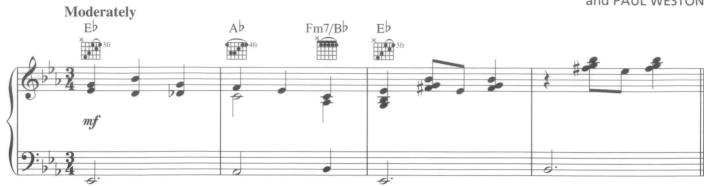

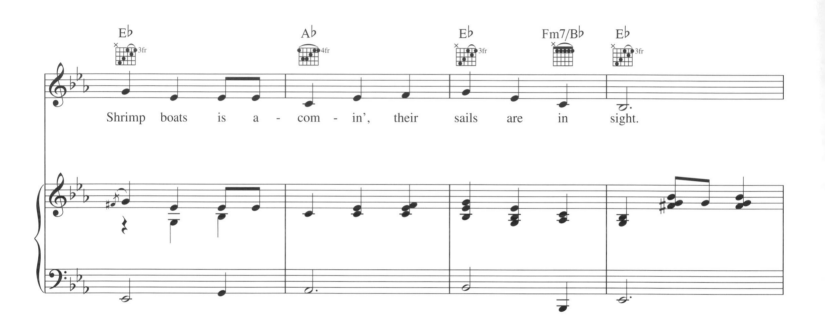

Shrimp boats is a-com-in', their sails are in sight.

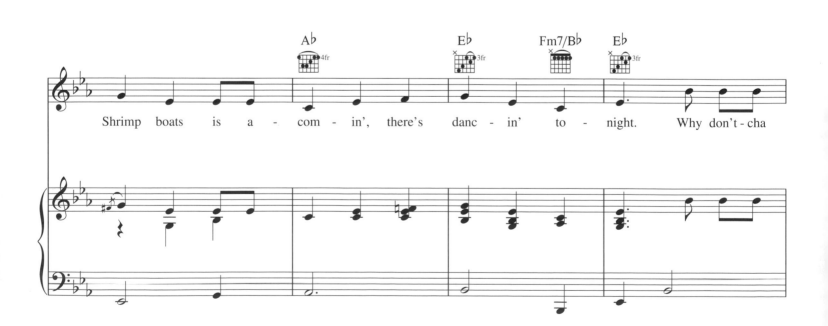

Shrimp boats is a-com-in', there's danc-in' to-night. Why don't-cha

hur - ry, hur - ry, hur - ry home, why don't-cha hur - ry, hur - ry, hur - ry home? (Look, here the)

Shrimp boats is a - com - in', there's danc - in to - night.

They go to sea with the eve - ning tide and their
Hap - py the days while they're mend - ing the nets 'til once

wom - en - folk wave their good - bye. _____
more they ride high out to sea. _____

SLOOP JOHN B.

Words and Music by PHIL F. SLOAN,
STEVE BARRI, BARRY McGUIRE and BONES HOWE

With a Calypso beat

We came on the Sloop John B., my
The first mate, he got so drunk, he
The cook went and got the fits, he

grand - fa - ther and me. 'Round Nas - sau town
broke o - pen my trunk. Poor sea - sick me
poured beer on my grits. In - to my soup

we did roam. Drink - in' all
on the foam. O - ceans are
went his comb. Oh, what a

SPLISH SPLASH

Words and Music by BOBBY DARIN
and MURRAY KAUFMAN

Moderately, with a beat

SMOKE ON THE WATER

Words and Music by RITCHIE BLACKMORE, IAN GILLAN,
ROGER GLOVER, JON LORD and IAN PAICE

We   all   came   out   to   Mon -
They   burned down   the gam -
We   end - ed   up   at the Grand

-treux on the Lake Ge-ne-va shore-line,
bling house, it died with an aw-ful sound.
Ho-tel, It was emp-ty cold and bare, but with the

to make rec-ords with the mo-bile. We did-n't
And funk-y Claude was run-ning in and out, pull-ing
roll-ing truck stones thing just out-side, mak-ing our

have much time. Frank Zap-pa and the Moth-ers were
kids out the ground. When it all was o-ver, we
mu-sic there. With a few red lights, a few old beds,

Repeat and Fade

Optional Ending

STORMY WEATHER
(Keeps Rainin' All the Time)

Lyric by TED KOEHLER
Music by HAROLD ARLEN

Don't know why _____ there's no sun up in the sky, storm-y weath-er, _____

Since my {man / gal} and I ain't to-geth-er, _____ keeps rain-in' all ___ the time. _____

Life is bare, _____ gloom and mis-'ry ev-'ry-where, storm-y weath-er, _____

SURFIN' U.S.A.

Words and Music by
CHUCK BERRY

THE TIDE IS HIGH

Words and Music by JOHN HOLT,
TYRONE EVANS and HOWARD BARRETT

Recorded a half step higher.

UNDER THE SEA
from Walt Disney's THE LITTLE MERMAID

Lyrics by HOWARD ASHMAN
Music by ALAN MENKEN

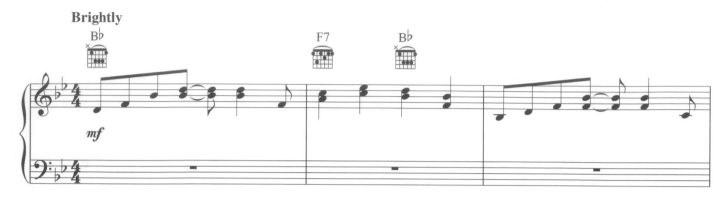

The sea - weed is al - ways green - er
Down here __ all the fish is hap - py

in some - bod - y else - 's lake.
as off __ through the waves dey roll.

You dream __ a - bout
The fish __ on the

SURF CITY

Words and Music by BRIAN WILSON
and JAN BERRY

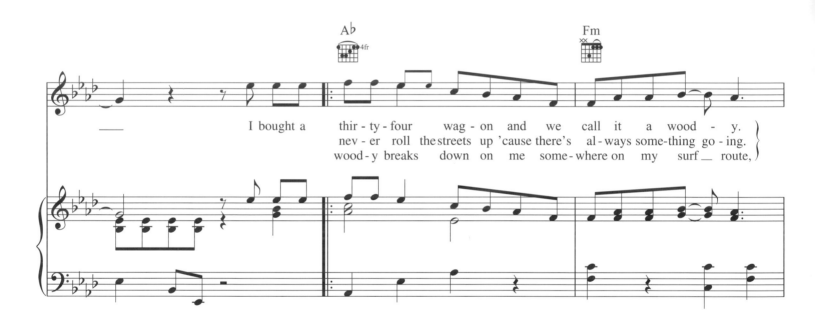

oh, that blow - fish blow.

Un - der the sea.   Un - der the sea.

When the sar - dine be - gin the be - guine, it's mu - sic to

sea.   Each lit-tle snail here know_ how to

wail here. That's_ why it's hot-ter un-der the wa-ter. Ya,_ we in

luck here down_ in the muck here un-der the sea._

WADE IN THE WATER

Traditional Spiritual

A WHALE OF A TALE

from Walt Disney's 20,000 LEAGUES UNDER THE SEA

Words and Music by NORMAN GIMBEL
and AL HOFFMAN

YELLOW SUBMARINE

Words and Music by JOHN LENNON
and PAUL McCARTNEY

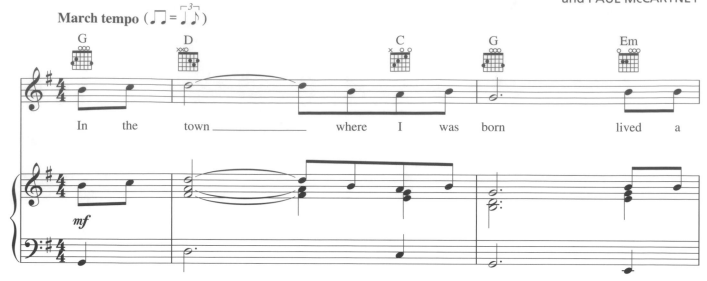

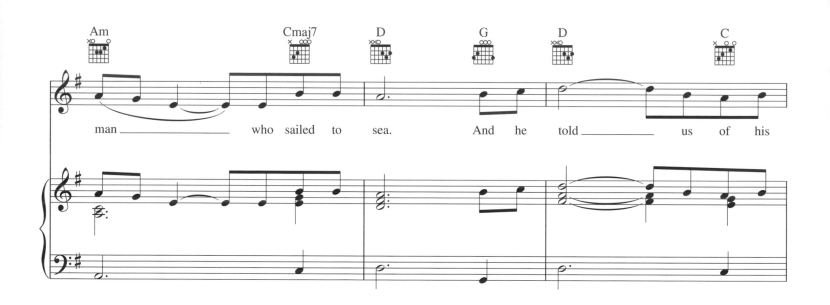

UNDER THE BOARDWALK

Words and Music by ARTIE RESNICK
and KENNY YOUNG

Moderately, with a beat

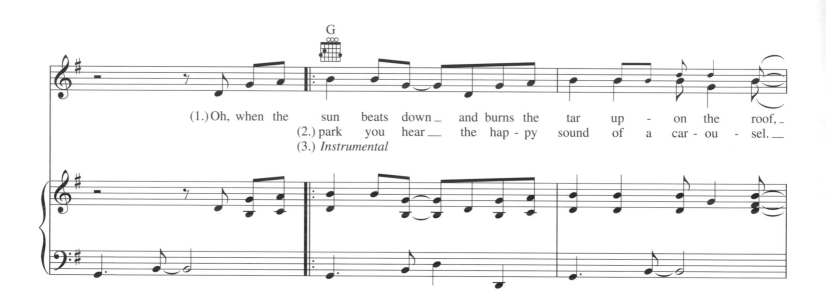

(1.) Oh, when the sun beats down __ and burns the tar up - on the roof, __
(2.) park you hear __ the hap - py sound of a car - ou - sel. __
(3.) *Instrumental*

_____ and your shoes get so hot   you wish your
_____ You can al - most __ taste   the hot